SHARKS

Shark Magic for Kids

To Joel Krauska and G. E. Smith and all kids who love sharks.
— Patricia Corrigan

For a free catalog describing Gareth Stevens Publishing's list of high-quality books and multimedia programs, call 1-800-542-2595 (USA) or 1-800-461-9120 (Canada). Gareth Stevens Publishing's Fax: 414-225-0377.
See our catalog, too, on the World Wide Web: http://gsinc.com

Library of Congress Cataloging-in-Publication Data

Corrigan, Patricia, 1948-
    Shark magic for kids / by Patricia Corrigan ;
  illustrations by John F. McGee.
      p. cm. -- (Animal magic for kids)
    Based on Sharks for kids. © 1995.
    Includes index.
    Summary: Information about sharks, plentifully illustrated.
    ISBN 0-8368-1633-1 (lib. bdg.)
    1. Sharks--Juvenile literature. [1. Sharks.] I. McGee, John F., ill.
II. Title. III. Series.
QL638.9.C635 1996
597'.31--dc20   96-16947

First published in this edition in
North America in 1996 by
Gareth Stevens Publishing
1555 North RiverCenter Drive, Suite 201
Milwaukee, Wisconsin 53212 USA

Based on the book, *Sharks for Kids*, text © 1995 by Patricia Corrigan, all photographs © 1995 Pacific Stock, except Bill Curtsinger, 11, 34, with illustrations by John F. McGee. First published in the United States in 1995 by NorthWord Press, Inc., Minocqua, Wisconsin. End matter © 1996 by Gareth Stevens, Inc.

Printed in the United States of America

1 2 3 4 5 6 7 8 9 99 98 97 96

by Patricia Corrigan

SHARKS

Shark Magic for Kids

Gareth Stevens Publishing
MILWAUKEE

You will not believe me when I tell you this, but it's absolutely true.

I've seen sharks—and lived! Actually, it was just one shark, but he could easily have killed me, eaten me alive.

Well, my uncle says sharks probably have no interest in eating people. I know now that he's right, but this shark sure looked like he could have eaten me alive if he wanted to!

My name is Gerald, and I'm 9. My Uncle Joe is a diver. Everywhere he goes, he wears a shark's tooth on a chain around his neck.

We visited him on our vacation, and he took me out on his boat one afternoon. We didn't do any diving, because I haven't learned how yet.

Out on the boat, we talked about the gulls flying overhead and the different kinds of fish in the water. Uncle Joe saw the shark first, and showed it to me.

He knew it was a blue shark because of its blue color and long, pointed nose. I saw the tip of its dorsal fin sticking up out of the water. I could sort of tell what its long, thin body looked like, though the water wasn't too clear.

I think I saw the shark's big eye!

One minute, the shark was cruising along, swimming near the surface. The next minute, it was gone. Uncle Joe said the shark was about 6 feet long—that's bigger than I am! Uncle Joe also said he's heard of blue sharks almost twice that big.

SHARK 3FT —O— 4FT METER 5FT 6FT

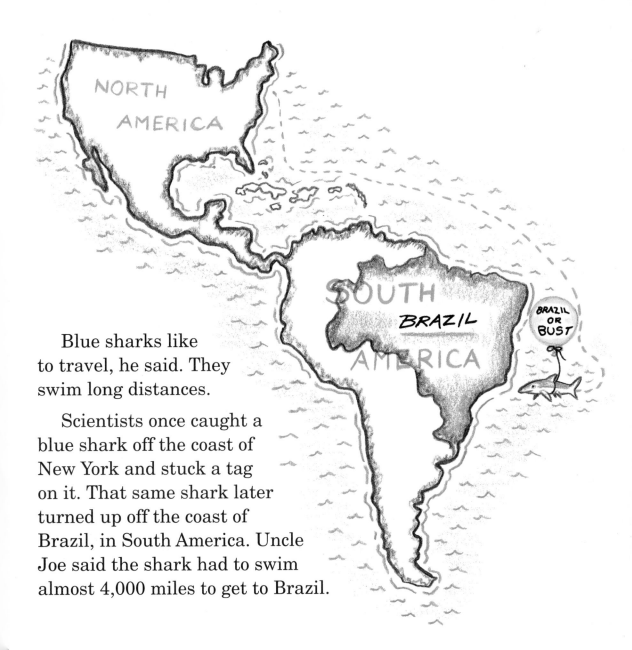

Blue sharks like to travel, he said. They swim long distances.

Scientists once caught a blue shark off the coast of New York and stuck a tag on it. That same shark later turned up off the coast of Brazil, in South America. Uncle Joe said the shark had to swim almost 4,000 miles to get to Brazil.

Blue shark

Like other sharks, blue sharks eat mostly fish and squid. Sometimes the sharks open their mouths wide and swim right through a bunch of squid or anchovies. Sometimes they sneak up on them from below.

Whale shark

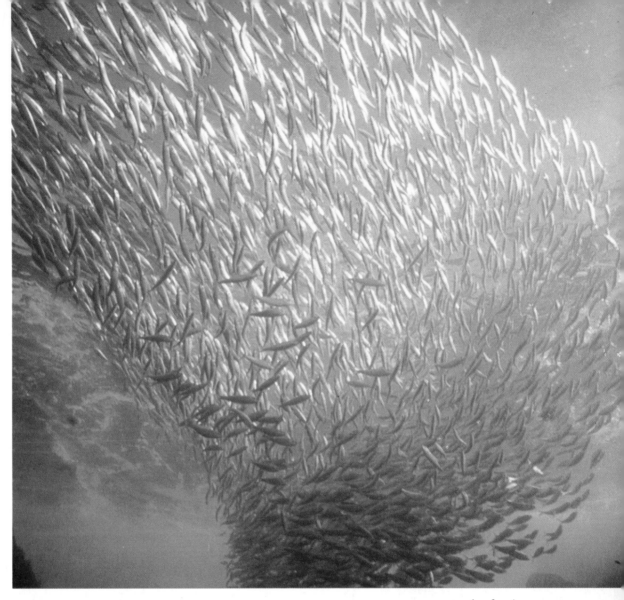

Anchovies

Guess what?

No matter how old they are or how many squid they've eaten, sharks always have enough teeth. I saw this on television, and Uncle Joe says it's true.

All sharks have several rows of teeth growing at once. Imagine hundreds of sharp teeth, all in your mouth at the same time.

Usually, only the front one or two rows stand up. As the shark loses those teeth, the teeth in the rows behind move forward and stand up, ready to go.

Some sharks lose one tooth at a time. Other sharks lose whole rows at once. Some sharks lose a whole row of teeth every week. Some lose a row every six months. Scientists think a single shark may lose as many as 30,000 teeth in a lifetime.

If sharks had tooth fairies, they would be busy!

Great white shark

Different species have different kinds of teeth. For instance, the sixgill shark has teeth that look like little saws, with serrated edges. The night shark has tall, pointy teeth. The oceanic whitetip shark has triangular teeth with sharp edges. And the horn shark's teeth are flat and blunt.

I saw a picture once of a shark called the cookie-cutter shark. These little sharks are only about 15 to 16 inches long. They have big round mouths and long sharp teeth. Cookie-cutter sharks open their mouths and attach themselves to their prey. Then they twist and turn their entire bodies round and round, carving out fat chunks of flesh.

Cookie-cutter sharks apparently fear nothing, and often go after large prey. How large? Well, some whales have been wounded by cookie-cutter sharks. Also, the U.S. Navy has reported finding cookie-cutter shark teeth marks on the rubber casings of equipment used outside of submarines!

Hammerhead shark

Uncle Joe says he wants to dive with hammerhead sharks. He drew me a picture of a hammerhead, and you'd know one if you saw one!

Hammerhead sharks have broad heads that look like a double-bladed axe. Their bodies range from about five to twenty feet long, depending on the type of hammerhead. Uncle Joe says some hammerhead sharks have smooth heads and some have scalloped heads. The biggest hammerhead is the great hammerhead. The smallest is called a bonnethead.

Every hammerhead shark has one eye and one nostril at either end of its head. Nobody knows why. But hammerhead sharks can probably see and smell better than other sharks.

Their favorite food is the stingray, which hides buried in the sand on the ocean floor. The stingray's sharp, poisonous barbs don't seem to bother the hammerheads. They eat them right up, barbs and all. Uncle Joe says hammerhead sharks usually swim slowly away when they see divers.

Before we left Uncle Joe's, he told my parents about an aquarium on the way home. He suggested we stop there. We spent a whole afternoon at the aquarium, and I went to a class on sharks for kids. I learned a lot.

Mrs. Remming, the teacher, wore a neat tee-shirt with sharks swimming all around it. She told us that sharks are fish. Most fish have bones, but sharks have cartilage. We have cartilage in our bodies too—our noses are made of cartilage, which is more flexible than bone.

Sharks have just the right equipment for living in the world's oceans, she said.

Whale shark with diver

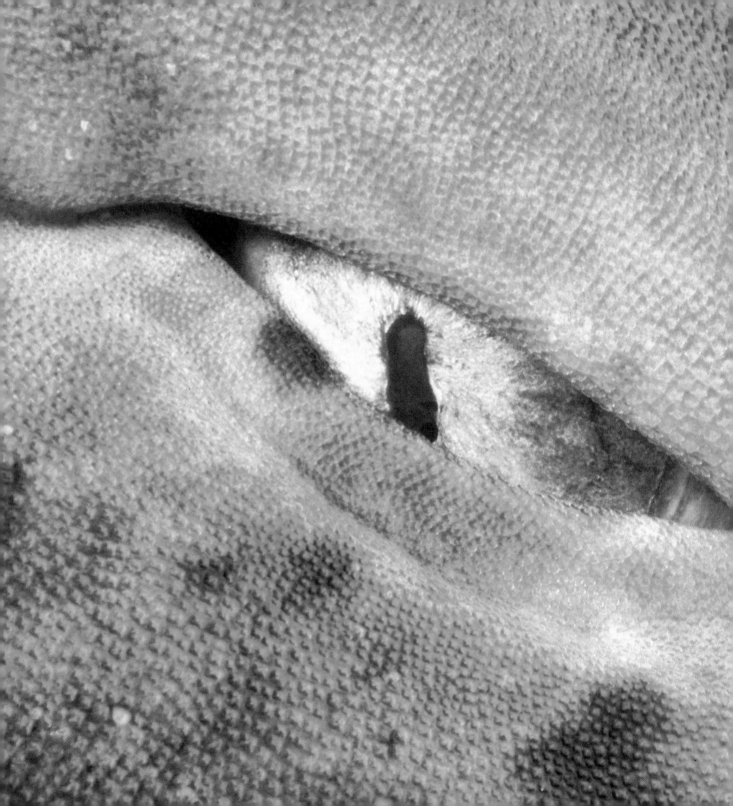

Sharks have good eyesight. Some sharks, such as the lemon shark and the great white, even have a third eyelid that protects the eye when the shark is hunting or feeding. Sharks hear especially well too. Their ears are inside their heads, connected to the outside by a tiny opening. Sharks also have a good sense of smell. They can smell food from great distances away, and they will follow the scent.

Another way sharks find food is through a special sensory system. It works like this: Each shark has hundreds of pores on its head. In pictures of sharks, you can see the pores under the snout. The pores are called ampullae of Lorenzini (That's pronounced AM-PEW-LIE of LORE-IN-ZEE-NEE).

Those pores detect electrical fields in the water. Mrs. Remming said that all living creatures produce electrical fields. Fish and stingrays can run from sharks, but they can't hide, because the sharks can sense them with the special pores.

Close-up view of a Nurse shark eye

Fish lay eggs, but sharks do not. Unborn sharks are called embryos (EM-BREE-OHS). Some embryos develop in eggs inside the mother's body. Those embryos are nourished by the egg until the baby sharks are born. Baby sharks are called pups.

Some sharks, such as the Port Jackson shark and the horn shark, produce an egg case that looks like a little leather pouch. Ancient Greeks called the pouch a "mermaid's purse." The mother shark deposits the eggs in the case. Then she puts the egg case in sea grass or in the sand on the bottom of the ocean. When the pups are born, they break out of the case.

Other sharks, such as the bull shark and the sandbar shark, give birth to live pups, which were nourished inside the mother by a placenta, just as in mammals. Some sharks bear just one pup; others have as many as 100.

Horn shark

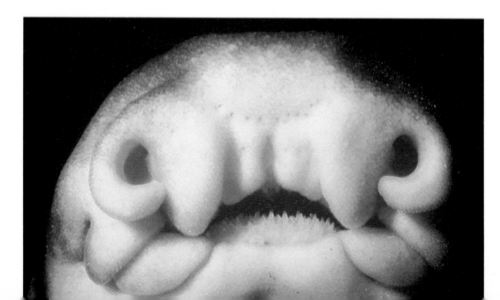

Fish have just one gill opening, but some sharks have as many as seven. When sharks breathe, water goes through their mouths, over their gills and out the gill openings.

Some people think sharks must swim in order to breathe. That's true for many sharks, but not for all of them. Some sharks, such as the lemon shark, spend a lot of time resting at the bottom of the sea, and they breathe just fine. Scientists are not sure if sharks ever sleep like we do. We do know that some sharks appear to slow down their breathing and remain still for a while.

Because they live under-water, sharks are hard to study. Scientists who study sharks are called elasmobranchologists (EE-LAZ-MOE-BRANK-OWL-OH-JISTS).

Nurse shark

Scientists say there are more than 350 different species of sharks. We don't know exactly how many there are, because new species are discovered every year. Scientists have sorted the sharks we do know about into eight major groups, or orders, based on their characteristics.

Sharks' official Latin names are often hard to pronounce, but many of them have wonderful common names. Mrs. Remming pointed out that a lot of the names appear to have been borrowed from other animals.

Here are some examples: cow shark, bull shark, cat shark, dogfish shark, leopard shark, bulldog shark, seal shark, zebra shark, crocodile shark, elephant shark, salmon shark, and tiger shark.

ELE

YOU CAN'T SEE ME!

Some sharks' names describe their appearance: sharpnose seven-gill shark, velvet belly shark, snaggletooth shark, daggernose shark, and silky shark.

A shark known as the nervous shark is said to hide its eyes with its tail when it's caught.

Swell shark

The goblin shark has pale white or gray skin. One shark is known as the swell shark, not because it's any neater than other sharks, but because it swallows water and swells up its body to protect itself.

I think all sharks are swell.

People have always been interested in sharks. Mrs. Remming said some islanders in the South Pacific once believed that sharks had magic powers. The islanders also cast spells and "called" the sharks. Sometimes the sharks came, she said.

Great white shark

The sharks' earliest relatives lived on Earth 350 million years ago. A giant shark that is now extinct weighed as much as 50,000 pounds and grew to 55 feet long. The shark's teeth were six to eight inches long! That shark was more than twice as big as the great white shark that lives today.

The biggest shark alive today is the whale shark, the largest fish on Earth. Whale sharks, which are bigger than many whales, may grow to 59 feet long. The biggest one ever measured weighed 80,000 pounds.

Even though they are very big, whale sharks are gentle. Some divers have grabbed their dorsal fins and swam right along with them. They live in warm, tropical seas.

Whale sharks are brown or gray, with lots of stripes and spots. Like some whales, they eat plankton or tiny krill.

Whale shark

Scientists have found weird things in whale sharks' stomachs. One whale shark had eaten a boot, a tin bucket, a wallet and part of a boat oar.

Scientists say all sharks can push their stomachs up toward their mouths and eject undigestible objects, such as turtle shells. Then the muscles pull the stomach back down.

I guess wallets are digestible—for sharks, anyway.

Close-up view of Krill

The smallest shark is the dwarf dogshark, which grows to about 6 1/2 inches. That's small enough to fit across a grown-up's hand. They live far beneath the Caribbean Sea.

Another small shark is the cigar shark, which is just a little bigger than a dwarf dogshark. A cigar shark looks like a swimming cigar, with eyes and a tail.

After our class, Mrs. Remming said she had a surprise for us. We walked to another part of the aquarium, to the touch tank. In it was a 14-inch nurse shark. Every one of us got to touch it!

Nurse sharks are brown, and they grow to eight or nine feet. They live in the western and eastern Atlantic Ocean and also in the eastern Pacific Ocean. In some parts of the world, nurse sharks are caught for food. Some are caught for their thick skin, which is made into leather for shoes.

Scientists have trained some nurse sharks in captivity. The sharks learned to push their heads against a target to get food. No one knows how long they live in the wild, but some nurse sharks have lived in aquariums for as long as 25 years.

Nurse shark

Mrs. Remming said not to touch the shark's head or gills—but she showed us how to stroke the shark's body. From front to back, the skin felt smooth. But from back to front, it was rough, like sandpaper.

That's because shark skin is made of little tooth-like scales, or denticles (DEN-TEE-KULLS). The denticles cover the shark's whole body. As the shark grows, it sheds its denticles and new, larger ones, grow.

As we took turns touching the shark, a girl came along who had not been in the class. She stepped up to the tank, looked at the little nurse shark, and said, "Wow! Sharks! They'll kill you."

That upset me, because I know that's not always true.

Great white shark

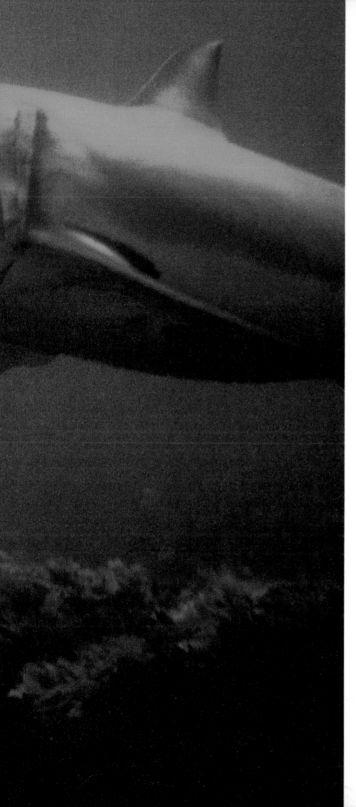

Some sharks have killed people. Some people believe that sharks attack people for food, but scientists say that's not true. People are not the preferred food of sharks. Some sharks that have attacked humans have actually spit them out and swam away.

Maybe we don't taste good to sharks.

Great white shark with diver

Sharks mainly eat fish, crabs, shrimps, squid, and some marine mammals. I read once that an entire reindeer was found in the stomach of a Greenland shark, but that was unusual.

Scientists say that about 65 sharks—fewer than 20 percent of all the sharks in the world—are dangerous. "Dangerous" means they might bite, though some of the smaller sharks have small teeth and can't really hurt you.

Of course, some of the dangerous sharks are not small, and they have large teeth. The four species that have harmed the most people are the great white shark, the tiger shark, the bull shark and the oceanic whitetip shark.

Whitetip shark

At times, sharks attack divers who harass them. Sharks may confuse the sound of people splashing in the surf with the sound of a school of fish. To sharks, a person paddling on a surfboard may look just like a sea lion. I think people who are afraid of sharks, or who say they hate them, don't understand sharks.

Sharks are vital members of the natural world. If they all died out, their prey would take over the oceans. Then, these animals would not be able to find enough to eat, and they would die, too. Sharks are a necessary part of the ecosystem.

Tiger shark

GLOSSARY

Denticles: Toothlike scales that cover a shark's body (page 40).

Dorsal: Near or on the back (page 6).

Ecosystem: The animals, plants, and nonliving things that make up an environment and that affect one another (page 47).

Elasmobranchologist: A scientist who studies sharks (page 25).

Plankton: Tiny plants and animals floating in the ocean that are eaten by many marine animals (page 32).

Species: A group of living things that have similar characteristics and that interbreed (page 14).

ADULT-CHILD INTERACTION QUESTIONS

These are questions designed to encourage young readers to participate in further study and discussion of sharks.

1. Do sharks have any natural enemies?
2. How are sharks adapted for life in the ocean?
3. Can any other animals detect electrical fields like the shark?
4. Where are whale sharks found?
5. How do scientists safely study dangerous species of sharks?
6. What do sharks in captivity eat?
7. Do sharks travel the ocean alone or in groups?
8. Do any species of sharks migrate?
9. How are sharks like fish? How are they different?

MORE BOOKS TO READ

Shark by Michael Chinery (Troll)
Shark by Miranda MacQuitty (Knopf)
Sharks by Ruth Berman (Carolrhoda)
Sharks by Gary Lopez (Children's World)
Sharks: Challengers of the Deep by Mary Cerullo (Cobblehill)
Sharks: The Perfect Predator by Howard Hall (Blake)
World of Sharks by Sarah Palmer (Random House)

VIDEOS

Sharks (PBS Video)
Sharks: The True Story (Live Home Video)